RACHEL ISADORA

VIKING

VIKING
Published by the Penguin Group
Penguin Putnam Books for Young Readers, 345 Hudson Street, New York, New York 10014, U.S.A.
Penguin Books Ltd, 27 Wrights Lane, London W8 5TZ, England
Penguin Books Australia Ltd, Ringwood, Victoria, Australia
Penguin Books Canada Ltd, 10 Alcorn Avenue, Toronto, Ontario, Canada M4V 3B2
Penguin Books (N.Z.) Ltd, 182-190 Wairau Road, Auckland 10, New Zealand

Penguin Books Ltd, Registered Offices: Harmondsworth, Middlesex, England

First published in 1999 by Viking, a member of Penguin Putnam Books for Young Readers.

1 3 5 7 9 10 8 6 4 2
Copyright © Rachel Isadora, 1999

LIBRARY OF CONGRESS CATALOGING-IN-PUBLICATION DATA
Isadora, Rachel.
ABC pop! / by Rachel Isadora.
p. cm.
Summary: Each letter of the alphabet is represented by illustrations in a pop art style.
ISBN 0-670-88329-8
1. English language—Alphabet—Juvenile literature. 2. Pop art—Juvenile
literature. [1. Alphabet.] I. Title.
PE1155.I85 1999 428.1—dc21 98-45690 CIP AC

Printed in Hong Kong
Set in Tahoma

A
AIRPLANE

B

BUILDINGS

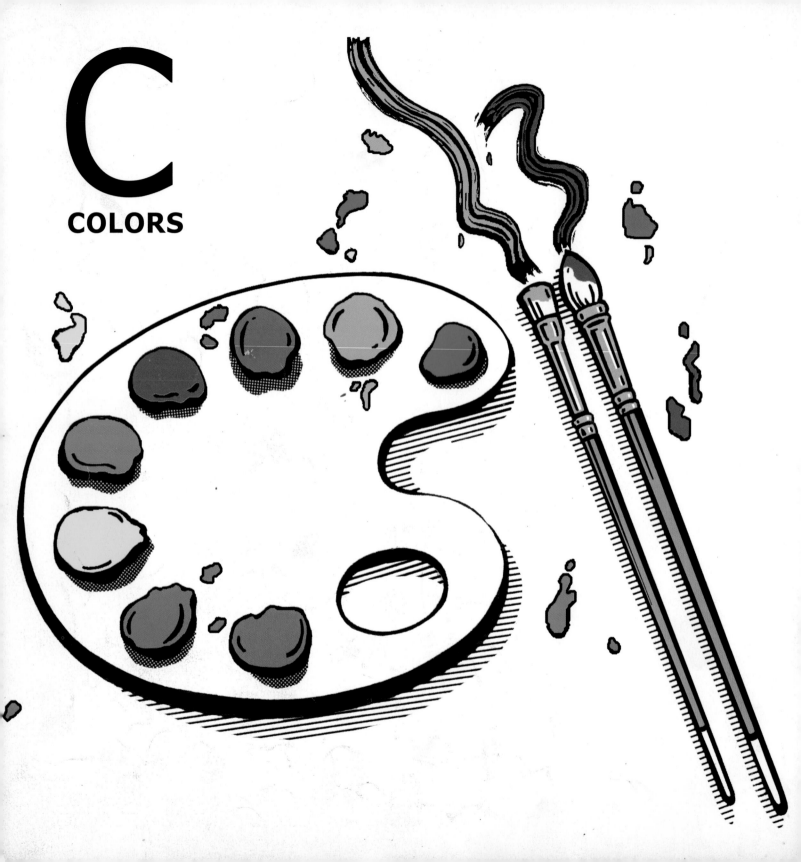

C
COLORS

D DANCER

E EGG

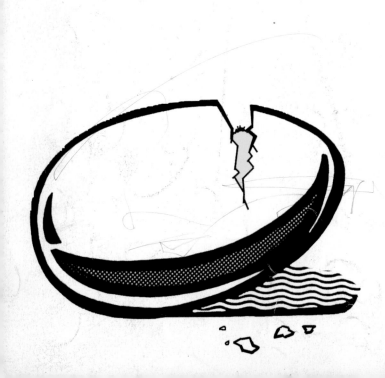

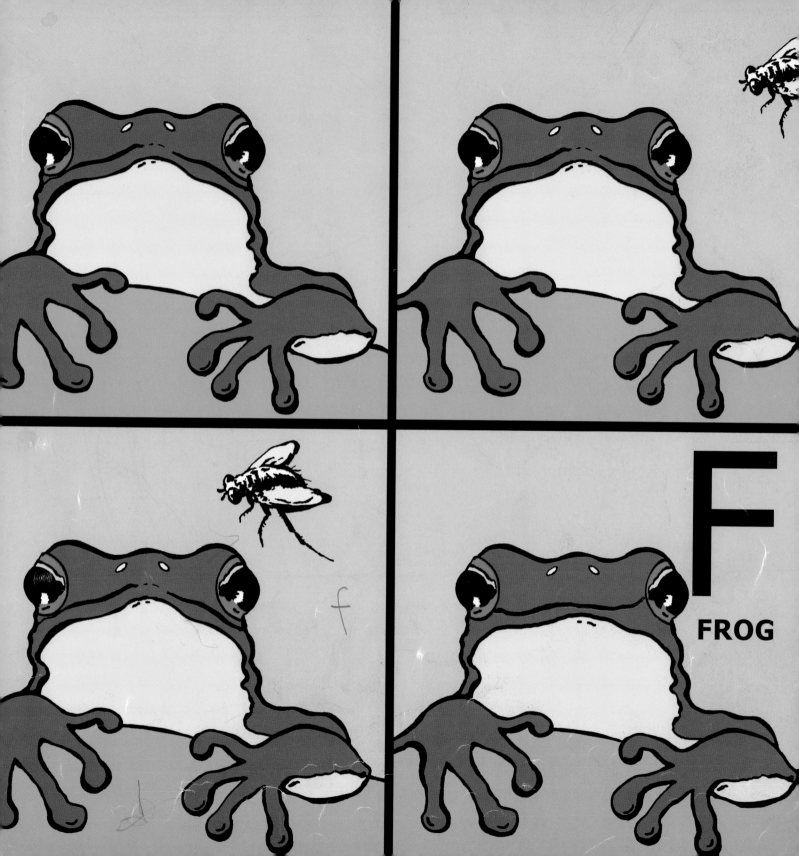

F

FROG

G

GAS

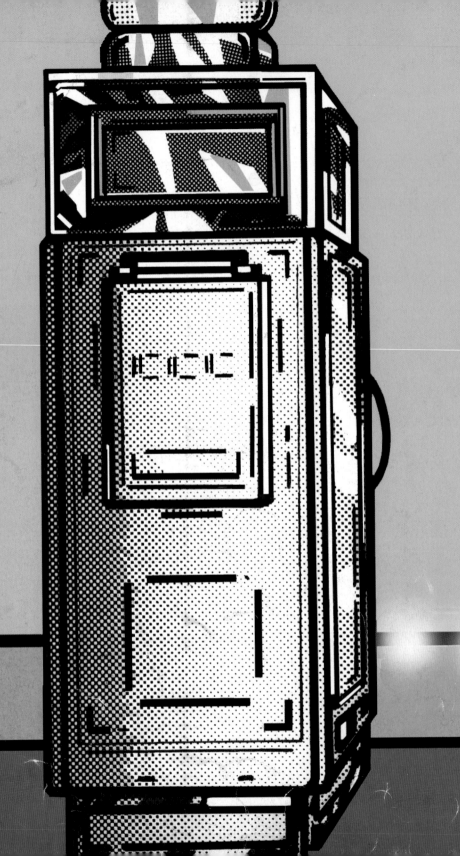

ICE

J

JACK-IN-THE-BOX

K KITCHEN

L

LOLLIPOPS

MUSIC

N

NOSE

OCEAN

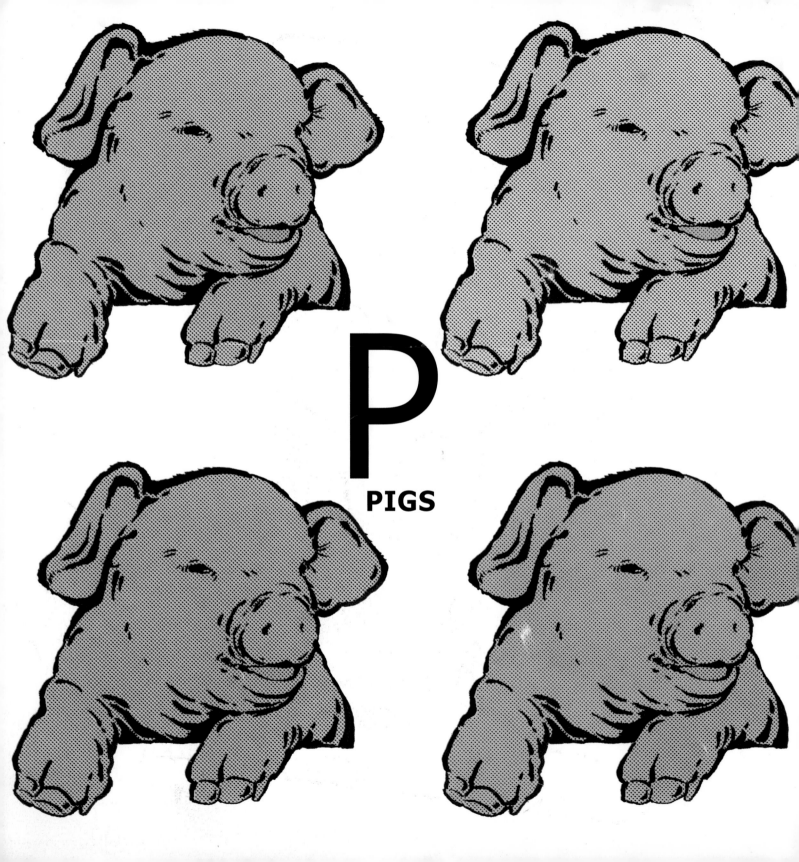

P

PIGS

Q

QUEEN

R

RATTLE

S

SUNDAE

T

TRAIN

V

VEGETABLES

W

WEB

X

XYLOPHONE

Y

YO-YO